This
Beltane Journal
Belongs To:

_____

Thanks for buying this journal!
I have lots more available on Amazon, including:

- Journals
- Undated Planners
- Composition Books (for school)
- Holiday themes
- Mermaids, Seahorses, starfish (I live near the beach, constant theme!)
- Florals & botanicals
- Hobby-themed journals for gardening, yoga, chakra-balancing, and other self-improvement topics – and some witchy stuff!

I'm Wanda, and Moon Magic Soul is my brand – welcome to my tribe!

Visit me:

www.moonmagicsoul.com

www.facebook.com/moonmagisoul

Using this Journal/Workbook

Welcome to the Season of Beltane!

The pages are a way for you to explore and celebrate the season – to document your thoughts and feelings about Beltane, and also to reflect on the past year, and keep moving through the new year!

Fill out what speaks to you – what you'd like to express. Ignore what doesn't fire you or interest you.

The first few pages are some month and week pages for personal planning. There are two months and six weeks – which gets you from Ostara to just past Beltane. If you already have a personal planner, you can art journal or ignore those pages.

Journaling – there are lots of journal prompts, have some fun with it! There are also some blank pages for you to doodle, scrapbook (paste or glue things) or make plans without lined pages.

Blessed be!

Sunday	Monday	Tuesday	Wednesday
☐	☐	☐	☐
☐	☐	☐	☐
☐	☐	☐	☐
☐	☐	☐	☐
☐	☐	☐	☐

MONTH

Thursday	Friday	Saturday
☐	☐	☐
☐	☐	☐
☐	☐	☐
☐	☐	☐
☐	☐	☐

Sunday	Monday	Tuesday	Wednesday

MONTH

Thursday	Friday	Saturday

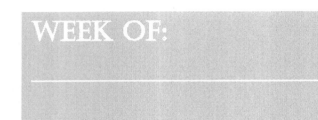

WEEK OF:

_____

Monday

Tuesday

Wednesday

Thursday

Friday

Saturday

Sunday

Notes

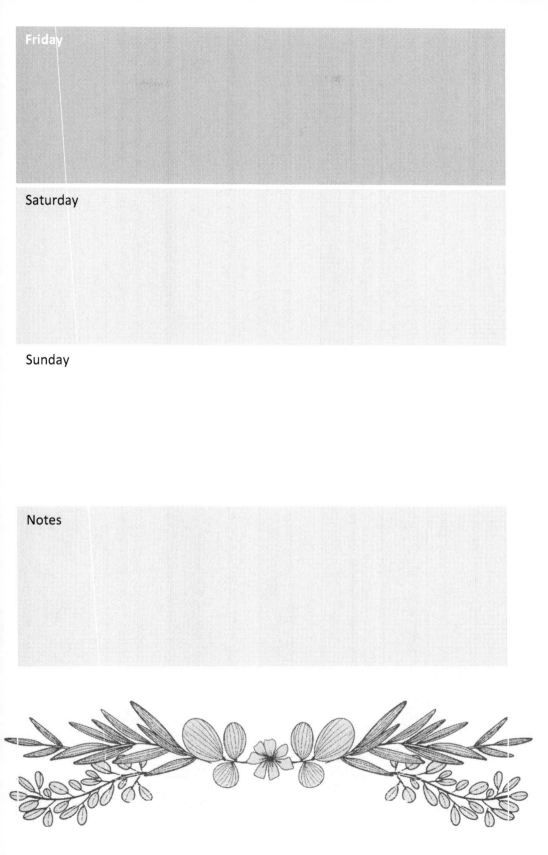

Monday

Tuesday

Wednesday

Thursday

Friday

Saturday

Sunday

Notes

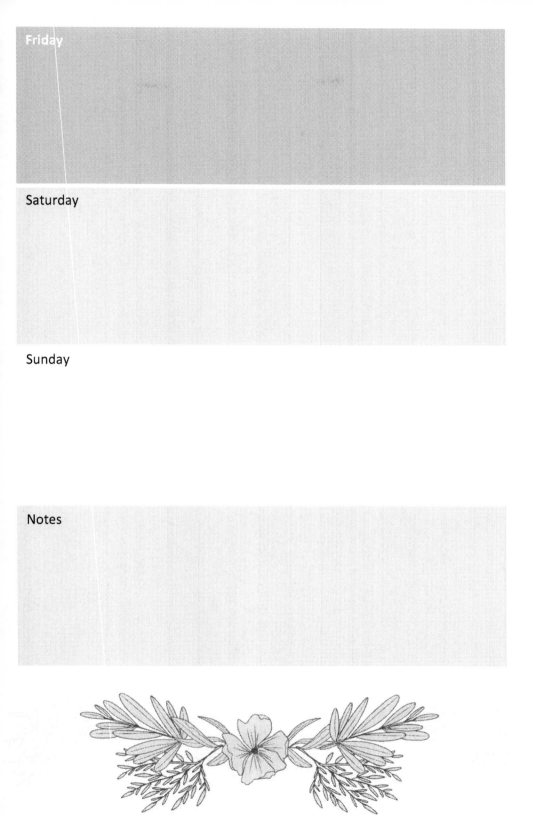

WEEK OF:

_____

Monday

Tuesday

Wednesday

Thursday

Friday

Saturday

Sunday

Notes

WEEK OF:

_____

Monday

Tuesday

Wednesday

Thursday

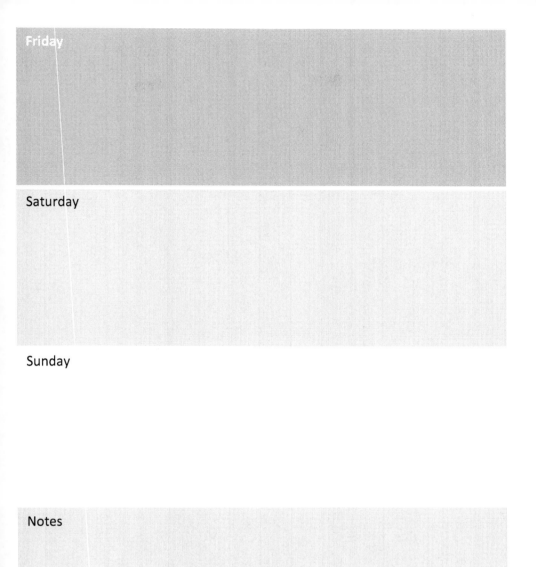

Friday

Saturday

Sunday

Notes

WEEK OF:

_____

Monday

Tuesday

Wednesday

Thursday

Friday

Saturday

Sunday

Notes

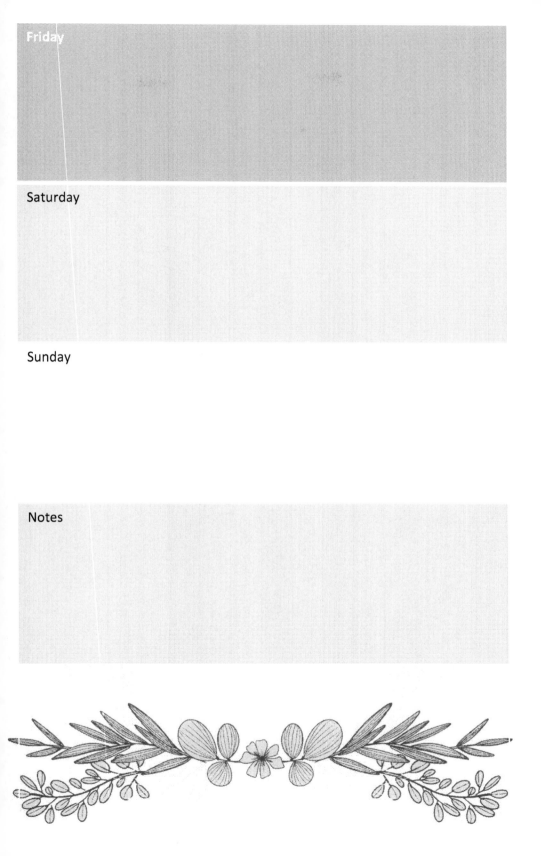

WEEK OF:

_____

Monday

Tuesday

Wednesday

Thursday

Friday

Saturday

Sunday

Notes

Meaning & Keywords

- ☐ A Wedding of the God and Goddess
- ☐ Bright Fire – Bonfires
- ☐ Fertility
- ☐ Many pagans choose this day for handfasting ceremonies

After celebrating Imbolc and Ostara, this time of the year celebrates the stirrings of spring come to full bloom! The fertility of the earth is on full display, and the intentions that you set back at Samhain and Yule are unfolding and unfurling and manifesting in beautiful ways!

Celebrate Beltane with happiness, and get outside and dance around a bonfire or in the beautiful moonlight!

How have you celebrated during the warming season since Ostara?

_____

_____

_____

_____

_____

_____

_____

_____

_____

_____

_____

_____

_____

_____

_____

_____

_____

_____

_____

_____

_____

How has your life changed since last Beltane?

What have you planted in your mind and your life?

How are your intentions growing and blossoming?

Have you planned or planted a summer garden yet?

_____

_____

_____

_____

_____

_____

_____

_____

_____

_____

_____

_____

_____

_____

_____

_____

_____

_____

_____

Scents of the Season

- ❑ Frankincense
- ❑ Jasmine
- ❑ Musk
- ❑ Peach
- ❑ Rose
- ❑ Vanilla
- ❑ Ylang Ylang

Scenting Your Home

- ❑ Incense
- ❑ Candles
- ❑ Essential Oils with Scent Sticks
- ❑ Essential Oils in Diffusers
- ❑ Essential Oils rubbed on air vents
- ❑ Commercial plugs (no judgment)

Beltane Essential Oil Diffuser Blend

If you haven't tried combining essential oils to scent your home and change your mood – here's a great recipe to start! Note how your thoughts change when using different essential oils and blends. If something gives you a headache – jot it down so that you know your triggers!

- ❑ 3 drops geranium.
- ❑ 3 drops ylang ylang.
- ❑ 3 drops jasmine.
- ❑ 3 drops frankincense

If you don't own a diffuser, you can put a drop of each oil on a tissue and attach it to an electric fan for a cheap homemade diffuser!

What scents make you think of the coming summer months?

_____
_____
_____
_____
_____
_____
_____
_____
_____
_____
_____
_____
_____
_____
_____
_____
_____
_____
_____

How do you plan to use scent this season?

Decorations

- ❑ Colors – Rainbow colors, dark and light green
- ❑ Acorns & blooming flowers
- ❑ Floral crowns and ribbon decorated baskets
- ❑ Maypoles, ribbon decorated rods and wreaths
- ❑ Bees, rabbits and doves

Do you decorate the entrance to your home to welcome the warmer weather?

_____

_____

_____

Do you decorate the living space of your home for spring and summer?

_____

_____

_____

What decorations are you seeing when you go out?

Have you planned any crafting to celebrate the season? What creative activities are you working through?

Foods

- ❏ Spring greens & salads
- ❏ Beltane Cakes & Biscuits
- ❏ Red/Pink Wines
- ❏ Cherries
- ❏ Dairy Foods & Beverages
- ❏ Honey
- ❏ Bread

Do you grow any food or herbs in your kitchen garden?

_____

_____

_____

Have you tried eating edible flowers?

_____

_____

_____

Idea – Try making breakfast burritos with eggs, cheese, tater tots and sautéed spinach or asparagus!

Beltane Biscuits

Preheat oven to 375 degrees, and combine:

4 cups sifted flour
1/2 cup ground almonds
2 cups sugar
1 tube almond paste
1/2 teaspoon baking powder
1 teaspoon cinnamon
5 eggs
½ cup powdered sugar
¼ teaspoon vanilla
1 – 2 teaspoons milk

1) Work dough into a medium soft ball, then divide into golfball-sized balls. Place on an ungreased cookie sheet and flatten with your hand or the bottom of a glass.
2) Bake until golden brown, about 20 minutes. Remove from oven and cool.
3) Mix powdered sugar, vanilla and 1 teaspoon milk in a small bowl. Use a spoon to drizzle a solar cross onto each biscuit!
4) You can also use a gluten-free biscuit mix for the base, and add sugar, cinnamon and cloves for flavoring.

What foods define the Beltane season for you?

What are your favorite salads and vegetables?

_____

_____

_____

_____

_____

_____

_____

_____

_____

_____

_____

_____

_____

_____

_____

_____

_____

Look up and list some Beltane recipes – and try them!

Celebrating Beltane in a group setting can satisfy your soul – how can you create a festive get-together for Beltane?

Activities for Beltane

- ☐ Set up your altar – use red and white candles, colourful wildflowers and crystals
- ☐ Take a walk outside – watch for and gather wand-sized fallen branches to make a new wand!
- ☐ Make a wand with items around your home – ribbon and cloth scraps, small jewellery findings, feathers and wire.
- ☐ Meditate outside – listen to the goddess
- ☐ Try weaving – make a potholder or a basket
- ☐ Make spiced wine or strawberry lemonade
- ☐ Set up a feeder for butterflies and bees
- ☐ Make a crown by weaving flowers
- ☐ Try maypole dancing, or decorate a rod with rainbow colored ribbon – lay on your altar!

What items are you using to decorate your altar?

How often do you re-decorate your altar?

Sketch a new plan for your altar setup here:

What quadrant of your altar is good for flowers?

Take a walk outside – notice the plant and animal life, and list what all you discovered!

_____

_____

_____

_____

_____

_____

_____

_____

_____

_____

_____

_____

_____

_____

_____

_____

_____

_____

_____

List the most notable moments that birds have gifted you with their feathers:

Thoughts On Wands

Wands have made a huge incursion with the fascination and decoration of the Harry Potter books and movies. There are some beautiful Pinterest images with gorgeous wands... Things to think about:

- Many of the gorgeous retail wands include hot glue, paste and paint, or are plastic-based. Be sure that you are comfortable with these processed items before purchasing.
- Making your own wand can be very satisfying and fulfilling – again, if you choose common crafting supplies, be sure that you're good with those choices. Chopsticks and hot glue can make some amazing and gorgeous wands.
- I prefer using malleable wire, beading and stones – more natural for my style.
- I also prefer to use gifted wood that has naturally fallen from a tree in my path. I don't use fresh-cut wood.
- I allow the branch to rest in my home for a couple of days before trimming and sanding. I will also oil the wood with whatever oil is handy – essential oils are nice too. I decorate wire with beading and wind around the wood, and attach stones with wire-cage constructs.

How often do you meditate? Have you tried any new meditation methods lately?

_____

_____

_____

_____

_____

_____

_____

_____

_____

_____

_____

_____

_____

_____

_____

_____

_____

_____

_____

_____

_____

Deities for Beltane

- ❑ Belenus/Balor
- ❑ Oak King
- ❑ Green Man
- ❑ Pan
- ❑ Cerunnos
- ❑ Maeve
- ❑ Tanit
- ❑ Flora
- ❑ Gaia
- ❑ Danu
- ❑ Herne

Do you have a particular deity that you work with during the spring/summer season?

How do you honor and thank the gods for the warmth of late spring and summer?

_____

_____

_____

_____

_____

_____

_____

_____

_____

_____

_____

_____

_____

_____

_____

_____

_____

_____

_____

Look up information about a deity you haven't met yet and write down what you find:

_____

_____

_____

_____

_____

_____

_____

_____

_____

_____

_____

_____

_____

_____

_____

_____

_____

_____

How often do you smudge yourself — and your home?

_____

_____

_____

_____

_____

_____

_____

_____

_____

_____

_____

_____

_____

_____

_____

_____

_____

_____

_____

How are you celebrating the Beltane season?

Spellwork & Rituals:

- ☐ Make an outdoor altar with green branches, flower blossoms, and other spring items
- ☐ Honor the wedding of the horned god and the goddess with offerings of wine, fruit and honey cakes
- ☐ Make a crystal grid in your garden with colourful flowers to attract fertility, abundance and other blessings
- ☐ Plant any seedlings that you began growing during Imbolc and Ostara, and ward them with protection to help your intentions grow and blossom
- ☐ If you don't already work with the moon phases, try a new ritual to set intentions with the New Moon, and set them free at the Full Moon.

List intentions that you set at Samhain and Yuletide. What are you contributing to manifest these intentions?

_____

_____

_____

_____

_____

_____

_____

_____

_____

_____

_____

_____

_____

_____

_____

_____

_____

_____

How have you honoured the Mother Goddess with new growth in your life this year?

Do you have a social group that you can celebrate the sabbats and esbats with? Why or why not?

Do you have a daily witchy practice to keep you in tune with the universe? List here – if not, develop one!

What are your favorite divination tools? Why?

_____

_____

_____

_____

_____

_____

_____

_____

_____

_____

_____

_____

_____

_____

_____

_____

_____

_____

_____

_____

Divination –
Looking Forward:

The next pages are spaces for you to record by month what your favorite divination tools are telling you about your upcoming year.

Make it a habit to review your reading on a monthly basis, and make comments about what has unfolded. Leave space in between for future journaling and exploration!

Month 1
The Season of Beltane

Month 1
Reflections

Month 2
The Season of Litha

Month 2
Reflections

Month 3
The Season of Summer

Month 3
Reflections

_____
_____
_____
_____
_____
_____
_____
_____
_____
_____
_____
_____
_____
_____
_____
_____
_____
_____
_____
_____
_____

Month 4
The Season of Lammas

Month 4
Reflections

_____

_____

_____

_____

_____

_____

_____

_____

_____

_____

_____

_____

_____

_____

_____

_____

_____

_____

_____

Month 5
The Season of Late Summer

Month 5
Reflections

Month 6
The Season of Samhain

Month 6
Reflections

Month 7
The Year Begins

Month 7
Reflections

Month 8
The Season of Yule

Month 8
Reflections

Month 9
The Season of Winter

Month 9
Reflections

Month 10
The Season of Imbolc

Month 10
Reflections

_____

_____

_____

_____

_____

_____

_____

_____

_____

_____

_____

_____

_____

_____

_____

_____

_____

_____

Month 11
The Season of Spring

Month 11
Reflections

Month 12
The Season of Ostara

Month 12
Reflections

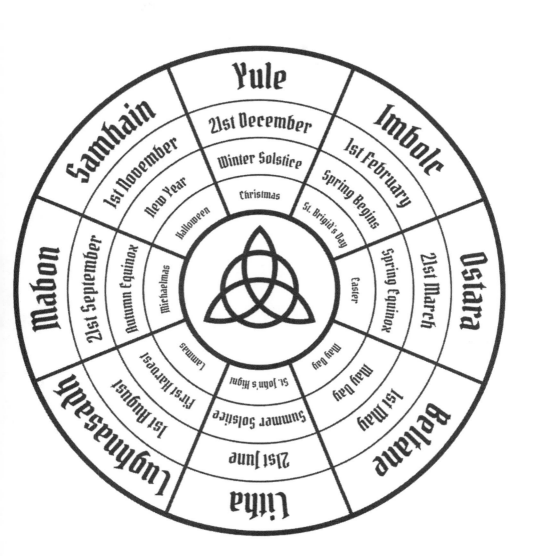

Thanks for buying this journal!
I have lots more available on Amazon, including:

- Journals
- Undated Planners
- Composition Books (for school)
- Holiday themes
- Mermaids, Seahorses, starfish (I live near the beach, constant theme!)
- Florals & botanicals
- Hobby-themed journals for gardening, yoga, chakra-balancing, and other self-improvement topics – and some witchy stuff!

I'm Wanda, and Moon Magic Soul is my brand – welcome to my tribe!

Visit me:

www.moonmagicsoul.com

www.facebook.com/moonmagisoul

Printed in Great Britain
by Amazon

79249016R30059